THE MONSTER STATES OF AM

1

F

1

ONE DOLLAR

THE MONSTER MONEY BOOK

THE
MONSTER MONEY BOOK

written and illustrated by Loreen Leedy

Holiday House   New York

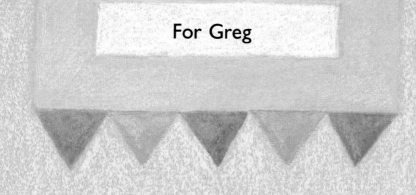

For Greg

Library of Congress Cataloging-in-Publication Data
Leedy, Loreen.
    The monster money book / written and illustrated by Loreen Leedy.
—1st ed.
        p.   cm.
    Summary: The members of the Monster Club discuss what to do with
the fifty-four dollars in their treasury.
    ISBN 0-8234-0922-8
    [1. Money—Fiction. 2. Clubs—Fiction. 3. Monsters—Fiction.]
I. Title.
PZ7.L51524Mo   1992   91-18168   CIP   AC
[E]—dc20
    ISBN 0-8234-1558-9 (pbk.)

More than anything in the world, Grub wanted to join The Monster Club. So he went to talk to his brother Spots, who was the president.

I hope you have some money for the meeting tomorrow.
To pay dues!
Why do we need money?
Every week the members pay dues to The Monster Club. We use the money for club projects.
I already spent my allowance. Can I borrow dues money from you?
Only if you pay it back.
Oh.
Maybe you could earn some money.

The next day, Sarah and Grub met the other members at the clubhouse.

The meeting began.

Let's start with the treasurer's report.

We have $54.00. Here are my numbers.

100 pennies	=	1 dollar
20 nickels	=	1 dollar
10 dimes	=	1 dollar
4 quarters	=	1 dollar
coins		4 dollars

10 ones	=	10 dollars
2 fives	=	10 dollars
1 ten	=	10 dollars
1 twenty	=	20 dollars
bills		50 dollars

$$\$4.00 + \$50.00 = \$54.00$$

How did you get so much money?
When we first started The Monster Club, we spent our dues money on candy every week.
We had piles of candy wrappers, but no money.
We wanted to do other things, like go to the movies and buy fuzzball equipment.
So we decided to start saving our money.
Have you spent any of it yet?
Today, we plan to decide what to spend it on.
We could go to the Monster Mall. There is so much to buy, it's hard to choose.

Let's buy toys!

Let's buy games!

How about pickles?

We should be careful not to waste money.

My mom told me to be a smart shopper.

Search for the lowest price, because stores have different prices.

Look for good quality. Poorly made things can fall apart.

Let's think of ways
to spend money that
will help the club!

How about paint for the clubhouse?

Wood for new steps!

A refrigerator!

Sarah stood up to ask a question.

Have you ever tried investing?

Hmmm, what's that?

Investing means to use money to make more money.

If you *spend* money on a glass of lemonade, and drink it up, the money is gone.

= 50¢

If you *invest* money in lemons and sugar, then sell lots of lemonade, you can make more money than what you started with.

The extra money is called a profit.

SUGAR

EXPENSES = $10.00

40 glasses X 50¢ = $20.00
expenses - $10.00
PROFIT $10.00

Oh, we did that for our car wash. We bought sponges and soap and wax and washed lots of cars. We made a profit of $20.00.

Spots held up his paw.

I've got another idea. Let's *give* some money away.

Why would we want to do that?

We could give money to someone who really needs it.
If we give money to a good cause, it will make the neighborhood better for all of us.
FOOD DONATIONS
THANK YOU!
CLEAN THE EARTH
RECYCLE
PLEASE GIVE
CARING FOR CRITTERS
I really need some money!
I said a *good* cause.

Loud voices rattled the clubhouse.

HOLD IT!

Great! Now that we know how to budget our money, let's get it out.
Do you keep it right here in the clubhouse?
Sure! It's over in the cookie jar.

The clubhouse is a terrible place to keep money!
Someone could steal it!

Money in the bank earns interest.

How interesting.

It is!

If you put $100.00 in a piggy bank at home, a year later you will still have $100.00.

If you put $100.00 in a bank savings account that pays 5% interest, a year later you will have $105.00.

Interest is extra money the bank pays while it uses your money.

What does the bank use our money for?

The bank lends money to people who need it. For example, someone might borrow money to buy a new house.

How do we get our money out of the bank when we want it?

You fill out a "withdrawal" form and give it to the person behind the counter or at the drive-up window.

You can also go to a bank machine.

You need a bank card and a secret code to get your money out.

WELCOME TO THE MONEY PLACE

The club members had one more thing to do.

GLOSSARY

Allowance: a sum of money received regularly, often once a week.

Bill: a piece of paper money.

Borrow: to receive money that will be paid back in the future.

Budget: a plan for using money.

Cash: paper money and coins.

Check: a printed piece of paper that, when filled out, allows one to withdraw money from a checking account.

Checking account: a sum of money placed in a bank by a person or group, which is spent when a check is written.

Coin: a small, flat, round piece of metal used as money.

Debt: an amount of money owed to a lender.

Donation: a gift of money to a person or group.

Dues: a sum of money paid to an organization by its members.

Earn: to receive money, usually for work.

Expense: how much something costs.

Interest: the extra money a bank pays a customer for the use of his or her funds.

Invest: to use money to make more money.

Lend: to provide money that must be paid back in the future.

Money: the coins and bills made by the government for people to trade for goods and services.

Price: the sum of money charged for a product or service.

Profit: the money left over after expenses have been paid.

Save: to keep money for future use, instead of spending it right away.

Savings account: a sum of money that earns interest from the bank.

Spend: to pay money for something.

Treasurer: the person who takes care of money for a group.

Withdraw: to remove money from a bank account.